Backyard
Bugs
& Creepy-
Crawlies

Wasps

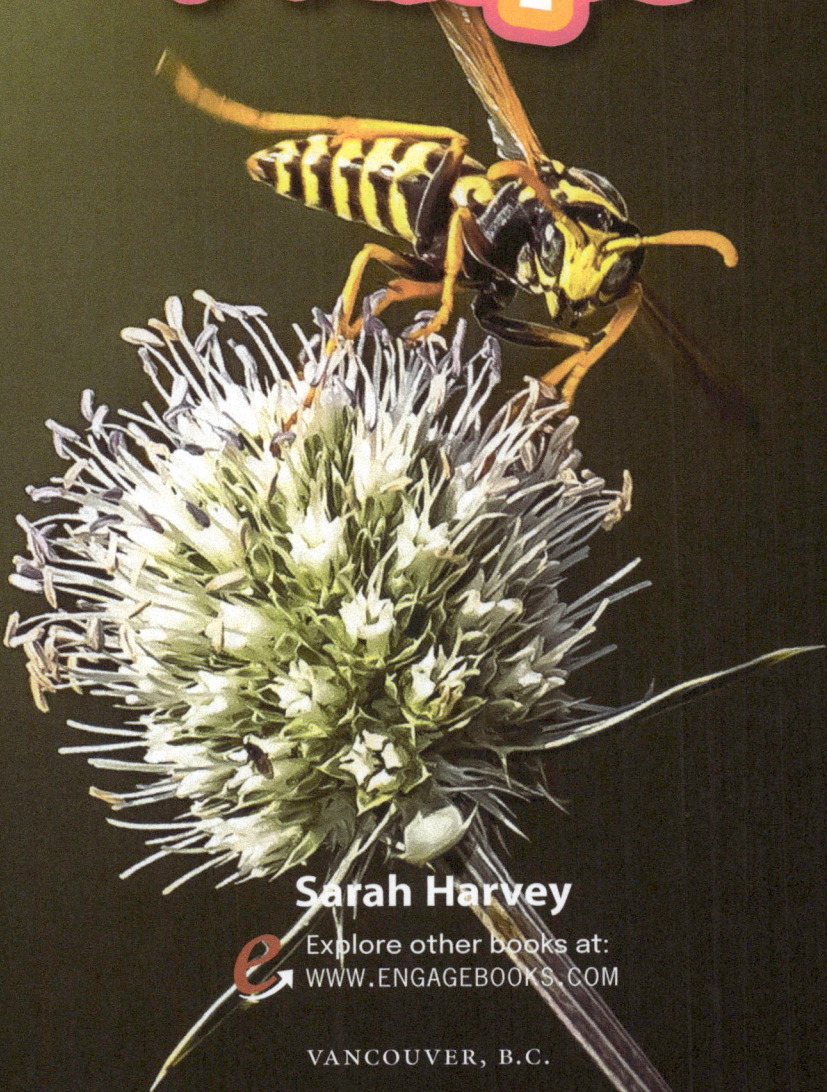

Sarah Harvey

Explore other books at:
WWW.ENGAGEBOOKS.COM

VANCOUVER, B.C.

e WWW.ENGAGEBOOKS.COM

Wasps: Level Pre-1
Backyard Bugs & Creepy Crawlies
Harvey, Sarah 1950 –
Text © 2022 Engage Books
Design © 2022 Engage Books

Edited by: A.R. Roumanis
and Sarah Harvey

Text set in Epilogue

FIRST EDITION / FIRST PRINTING

LIBRARY AND ARCHIVES CANADA CATALOGUING IN PUBLICATION

Title: Wasps / Sarah Harvey.
Names: Harvey, Sarah N., 1950- author.
Description: Series statement: Backyard bugs & creepy-crawlies
Engaging readers: level pre-1, beginner.

Identifiers: Canadiana (print) 20220403392 | Canadiana (ebook) 20220403406
ISBN 978-177476-700-9 (hardcover)
ISBN 978-177476-701-6 (softcover)
ISBN 978-177476-702-3 (epub)
ISBN 978-177476-703-0 (pdf)

Subjects:
LCSH: Wasps—Juvenile literature.

Classification: LCC QL565.2 .H37 2022 | DDC J595.79—DC23

This project has been made possible in part
by the Government of Canada.

Canada

Don't swat that wasp!

Wasps are insects.

Wing

Stinger

Legs

Antennae

Eye

Mouth

Only female wasps have a stinger.

The most common garden wasps are paper wasps, yellowjackets, and hornets.

Paper wasps have long, thin bodies.

Yellowjackets are brightly coloured.

Hornets are bigger than other wasps.

Wasps have little or no hair on their bodies.

Many wasps live
with other wasps
in large nests.

Some wasps live alone and make small nests.

Wasps chew up wood to make their nests.

Female wasps called queens build nests in the spring.

Queen

Queens lay eggs in cells in their nests.

Cell

Egg

Wasps hunt garden pests.

This helps keep plants healthy.

Like bees, wasps carry pollen from flower to flower.

They do not
make honey.

Wasps like rotten fruit, and sweet food and drinks.

Bright colors and strong smells attract wasps.

Sometimes wasps think their nest is under threat.

This makes them angry, and they may sting.

Never, never poke our nest!

Explore other books in the Backyard Bugs & Creepy Crawlies series!

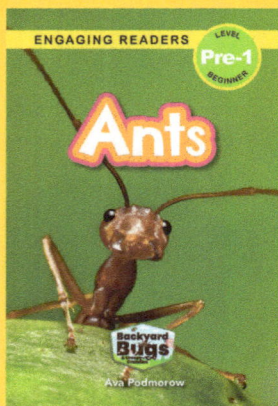

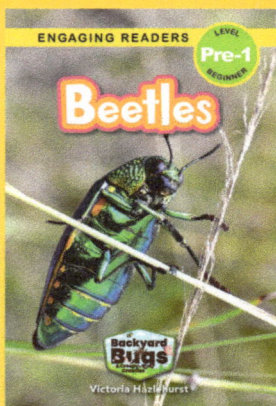

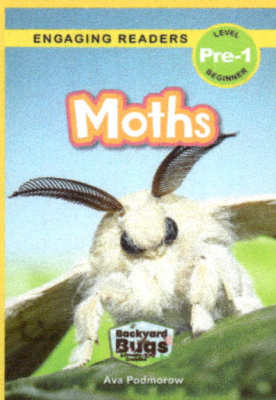

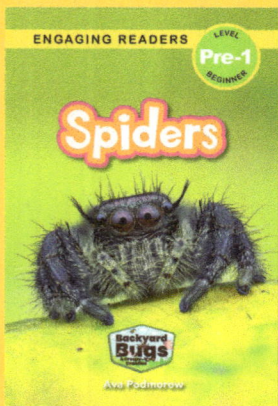

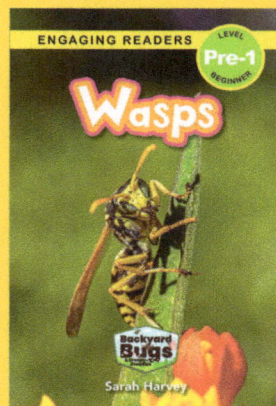

ENGAGING READERS — LEVEL Pre-1 BEGINNER
Ants
Backyard Bugs
Ava Podmorow

ENGAGING READERS — LEVEL Pre-1 BEGINNER
Beetles
Backyard Bugs
Victoria Hazlehurst

ENGAGING READERS — LEVEL Pre-1 BEGINNER
Caterpillars
Backyard Bugs
Ava Podmorow

ENGAGING READERS — LEVEL Pre-1 BEGINNER
Grasshoppers
Backyard Bugs
Ava Podmorow

ENGAGING READERS — LEVEL Pre-1 BEGINNER
Moths
Backyard Bugs
Ava Podmorow

ENGAGING READERS — LEVEL Pre-1 BEGINNER
Snails
Backyard Bugs
Ava Podmorow

ENGAGING READERS — LEVEL Pre-1 BEGINNER
Spiders
Backyard Bugs
Ava Podmorow

ENGAGING READERS — LEVEL Pre-1 BEGINNER
Wasps
Backyard Bugs
Sarah Harvey

ENGAGING READERS — LEVEL Pre-1 BEGINNER
Worms
Backyard Bugs
Victoria Hazlehurst

Explore books in the Animals In The City series.

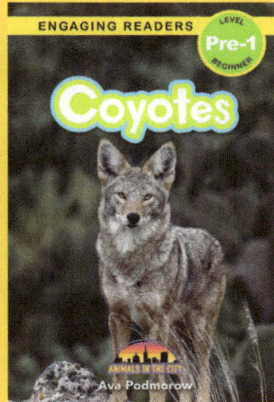

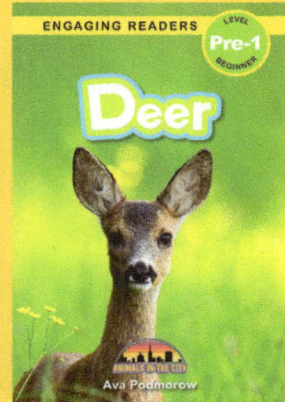

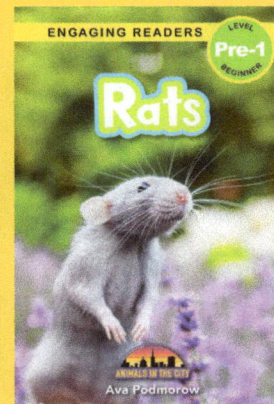

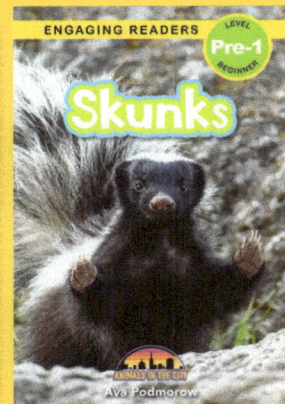

ENGAGING READERS — LEVEL Pre-1 BEGINNER

Cats
Ava Podmorow

Coyotes
Ava Podmorow

Deer
Ava Podmorow

Owls
Ava Podmorow

Pigeons
Ava Podmorow

Rabbits
Ava Podmorow

Raccoons
Sarah Harvey

Rats
Ava Podmorow

Skunks
Ava Podmorow